Philosophy for children

From child to children

Once upon a time!

Beauty is in the eye of the beholder!

Coloring story!

By: Bernardo Octaviano Pereira

This book belongs to:

____

I dedicate this work, firstly, to my parents who I love so much, to my teachers, to my dear aunts and to all my friends, may God bless you all infinitely!

Bernardo Octaviano Pereira

13/04/2024

I dedicate this work, firstly, to my parents who I love so much, to my teachers, to my dear aunts and to all my friends, may God bless you all infinitely!

@Bernardo6883©

Once upon a time, in a city near here, there lived a very pessimistic boy, he thought everything was ugly, wrong, boring, he didn't like anything or anyone;

He was always complaining about everything, his house was small, his car was old, the weather was always bad, the trees didn't bear fruit, nothing was good for him;

This pessimistic young man had a twin brother, completely opposite to his worldview. The optimistic brother appreciated every detail of life, expressed gratitude to the Creator for all things

The optimist's life was full of friends, as his positive attitude attracted people who valued his enlightened view of the world.

While the pessimist complained about the size of the house, the optimist celebrated each cozy space. While the pessimist lamented the age of the car,

the optimist remembered the adventures in each kilometer driven, the weather always beautiful, the trees always beautiful, full of flowers and fruits;

On a special day, while they both admired the sunset, the pessimist could only see dark clouds, but the optimist marveled at the golden tones that colored the sky.

One saw everything with criticism, and the other with love, not everything is perfect in this life, but beauty is in the eye of the beholder!

If we look critically, we will see that everything is wrong, but if we look with love we will see that everything is perfect.

This story reminds us that often how we choose to see the world shapes our experience.

If we adopt a more positive outlook, even in the face of imperfections, we can discover the beauty that exists in every moment and in every detail of life.

The end!